SLANG

ROBERT LAIDLER
MARK HARVEY

Crombie Jardine
PUBLISHING LIMITED

Crombie Jardine Publishing Limited
Unit 17,
196 Rose Street,
Edinburgh,
EH2 4AT
www.crombiejardine.com

First published by Crombie Jardine Publishing Limited, 2006

Copyright © Robert Laidler and Mark Harvey, 2006

ISBN 1-905102-85-2 (10-digit)

ISBN 978-1-905102-85-3 (13-digit)

Written by Robert Laidler and Mark Harvey
Designed by www.glensaville.com
Printed and bound in Great Britain by
William Clowes Ltd, Beccles, Suffolk

CONTENTS

THANKS

Our kind thanks go to the following individuals for their support, inspiration and contributions:

Ewan R Murray

Dot Morrison

Lesley Laidler

Michael Doherty

Ian McCartney

Robert Mitchell

James Blair

Derek Irvine

Graham Bell

Lis Dick

Grant Brodie

Douglas Stein

Mark Thomson

Emma Jane Stirling

Keith Skakle

Malcolm Bell

Neil Pollard

Nigel Harding

Tony Farrugia

Robert Laidler and Mark Harvey, 2006

INTRODUCTION

Perhaps boy scout will come o this but when we made a braveheart and put but 'n' ben tae paper we thought it'd gie somebody a laugh, even if it wis jist oorsels. We soon foun' it a Willie Waddle tae think o mair tae write, an' noo it's lookin' Gordon Strachan. We took Willie Wallace frae the fact that yin publisher didnae jist flush it doon the Steely Dan. Noo here we are hopin' that the Frank MacAvennie drops and youse oot there cullen skink that this is a guid idea. Enjoy the Tam O' Shanter, noo 'am aff fur a Single Fish.

Welcome to the world's first comprehensive guide to Scotland's own take on the slang language that Cockneys thought they'd made their own. This Highland view will once more send them homeward tae cullen skink again.

THE ORIGIN OF RHYMING SLANG

When Robert the Bruce returned to Scotland from Ireland in the early part of the 14th century he endured a torrid ferry crossing and then began the long process of claiming his right to the Scottish throne. This of course culminated in him defeating Edward II at Bannockburn in 1314 and a Scottish legend was born forever.

In the lead up to his triumph it is a mythological fact that in a dark Hebridean cave Robert gazed admirably at a spider weaving its' web. This gave him the belief that nothing was beyond his reach. What is not so well known is that, as the spider was his only companion at this time, he didn't like to leave the cave without letting the spider know where he was going. On one of these occasions he etched onto the cave wall the immortal words, "Ah'll be back in a meenit, jist awa' tae the caramel log fir a single fish." Little did he know it, but that day another legend was born, the legend of Jockney Rhyming Slang.

Over 400 years passed and not one other soul had entered that cave until Dr Samuel Johnson chanced upon it when seeking shelter during a storm on his tour of Scotland in 1773. Intrigued by the strange writing on the cave wall he noted Robert the Bruce's words down in his diary and asked his Scottish companion James Boswell to interpret them. He instantly warmed to this subtle use of substituting alternative similar sounding words for common objects and actions. Back in London Dr Johnson told friends of his discovery and they began to create their own examples of Rhyming Slang. Over the following century this slowly developed into the Cockney version of the Scottish original. Just another example of a great Scottish invention unscrupulously exploited by a nation with a lack of inspiration.

JOCKNEY RHYMING SLANG A-Z

ABERDEEN – MEAN

Considering most of the buildings are
made from granite, surely not?
"Gie the wean a tenner and stop being
so Aberdeen ya big dumplin'."

ABERFOYLE – OIL

Make sure that perfect family picnic to the
Trossachs doesn't give everyone a breakdown.
"Ya flamin' idiot! Ah telt ye tae
check the Aberfoyle afore we left."

ACME WRINGERS – FINGERS

Working in the factories of yesteryear,
one small slip around the mangle could
mean you never had to buy gloves again.
"Ah never knew that stove wiz oan. Ah've
burnt ma acme wringers so ah huv."

ALAN HANSEN – DANCIN'

The ex Sauchie and Liverpool man was
a fleet-footed defender who seemingly
could stroll through a game without
breaking sweat. Could he waltz
across a ballroom floor as easily?
"Com' oan, the taxi's waitin'. We're
gonnie be late fir the Alan Hansen."

ALAN ROUGH – GUFF

Scotland's performance in the 1978
World Cup was generally considered
an abject failure. The players' perms
should have been outlawed too, before
they even set foot in Argentina.

"Why dae we come here every week?
It's just a pile o'Alan Rough."

ALAN WELLS – SMELLS

I'm sure that Scotland's finest ever
sprinter always showered after racing.
However, there are people who like
to dodge the soap and water.

"Dinnae go near that guy,
he totally Alan Wells."

ALEXANDER GRAHAM BELL – TELL

When he invented the telephone, Mr
Bell could never have foreseen the late
20th century phenomenon of tabloid
editors receiving juicy gossip involving
a myriad of well kent public figures.
"See her, she Alexander Graham Bells
all, takes the money and runs."

ALLY MCCOIST – MOIST

Although never in the band, I'm sure many
female fans will always think of Ally first
when 'Wet, Wet, Wet' is mentioned.
"That's a lovely fruit loaf maw.
It's really very Ally McCoist."

ALLY MCLEOD – LOUD

The great prophet was never quite
the same man after the World Cup
debacle. Some things really shouldn't
be shouted from the rooftops.
"Hey pal, turn the music down.
It's a bit Ally McLeod."

ARMADILLO – PILLOW

The mini Sydney Opera House certainly
has startling sound qualities, but suffice
it to say there's been the odd band
or two over the years with that extra
quality of putting you to sleep.
"Ma heid just hit the Armadillo.
I wiz oot like a light."

ARTHUR'S SEAT – FEET

Wouldn't it be handy if there was a pair of baffies to slip into for those aching bunions.

"Ah must huv walked a marathon today. My Arthur's Seat are loupin'."

AULD REEKIE – FREAKY

Edinburgh's had its fair share of ghosts and ghouls over the years but sometimes a bit too much make-up might still provoke a comment.

"Clock the napper on that – Auld Reekie or what!?"

AYRSHIRE MIDDLE – FIDDLE

The police enjoy a bacon roll like the rest of us but they can't stomach benefit fraud.
"Jist whit's the Hampden Roar here big man, ah hope yer no on the Ayrshire Middle again pal."

BARLINNIE – MINI

Probably not the best choice of car to make your getaway in if you're planning to break out en masse.
"How many folk can ye actually squeeze in tae yer barlinnie?"

BASS ROCK – COCK

With the threat of bird flu looming large
on the horizon, the humble chicken
faces an uncertain future, but down
on the farm there is one wake up call
on which we can all still depend.

"A wiz up at 5.30 again cos o' that Bass
Rock crowing fir Scotland again."

BAY CITY ROLLERS – MOLARS

Nobody enjoys a trip to the dentist,
and often trying to hold a conversation
afterwards is also not recommended.

"Dinnae even try tae talk to me, 'ave jist
had twa o ma Bay City Rollers takin' oot."

BAYNE & DUCKETT – BUCKET

Today, if kids were shining shoes on the
side of the street they would probably be
contravening various Health and Safety
regulations. Oor Wullie would have a fit.
"Go and take the Bayne & Duckett
oot son, there's a good lad."

BEN NEVIS – CREVICE

Britain's highest peak is home to many
nooks and crannies and it's strange
how many times so many objects find
their way into those obscure places.
"Och no 'ave dropped ma hoose key
an' its gang doon yon Ben Nevis
by the side o the door step."

BERTI VOGTS – GOATS

The much maligned ex-Scotland manager probably thought the whole world was against him. As Alan Hansen once famously said, "You'll never win anything with kids."

"Nae wunner we didnae win the day. Ye aw played like a bunch o' Berti Vogts."

BERWICK UPON TWEED – HEID

A Scottish town in England – now that's a mind bender if ever there was one! Almost as challenging as a flat pack from Ikea in fact.

"See this self assembly lark, a can never get ma Berwick upon Tweed roon it."

BILL MCLAREN – SALMON

This unassuming rugby man certainly never went fishing for compliments during his broadcasting career. However, now he's deep into retirement, maybe he should hot rod it down to the local river and try a new pastime.

"That wiz a braw meal darlin', a real lovely piece o' Bill McLaren."

BILL SHANKLY – FRANKLY

The greatest post-war motivator of pre-prima donna football stars never gave a damn, just as long as one sacrificed oneself for the cause on the playing field.

"Football's no aboot life an' death, Bill Shankly it's mair important than that."

BILLY BUNTER – GRUNTER

Term mainly used in the west central belt of Scotland to describe a not very attractive girl.
"Look at the state o her,
whit a Billy Bunter."

BILLY SLOAN – GROAN

The Daily Record's very own pop mogul must have got exasperated a few times during his weekly exclusive interviews with the who's and the who's not of the music world.
"Am daeing ma best. Stop
geeing it big Billy Sloans!"

BLACK WATCH – SCOTCH

One of Scotland's finest and proudest

regiments didn't need any Dutch courage in the heat of battle, they were brave enough to handle the enemy with clear heads. A wee victory celebration afterwards though was always welcome. "Make mine a double Black Watch please bartender, it's been a long hard day oot there."

BLYTHE DUFF – MUFF

The Taggart investigative team are often caught up in Glasgow's dark underbelly, and then things can get just a little bit hairy. "Am aff fir a wax afore ma holidays cos ye can see ma Blythe peekin' o'er the tap o ma bikini boattams."

BOAT 'O' GARTEN – FARTIN'

Bird watching can be a painstaking business, and sometimes a little smelly too in a small hide...

"Whit's that stink, have you been Boat o Garten again? Ye'll need tae stop eatin' they kebabs."

BOY SCOUT – NOWT

One can only assume that Lord Baden Powell was a dab hand at needlework when he was a nipper. How else would he have got the idea of having to sew on badges the length of your arm for carrying out the most menial of tasks.

"I'll tell ye somethin' for nothin'. Yer no' gettin' another penny fi me, absolutely boy scout."

BRAVEHEART – START
With Mel Gibson starring in it, this was never going to be slow getting off the ground.
"Ye need to get a right guid Braveheart if ye're gonnae win this race."

BRIDGE O WEIR – QUEER
Grannies often come out with the most memorable quotes. I remember watching telly in 1984 when Freddie Mercury was hoovering his front room in Queen's famous pop video.
"A grown man singin' and daen hoosework tarted up like a wumman, dae ye no think yon's a wee bit Bridge o Weir?"

BRISTOL CHANNEL – PANEL (CHILDREN'S PANEL)

Teenagers can often be a handful, and on occasions some go a little too far – that is when the local authorities get involved.

"Aye it wiz arson by the way, 'an noo he's up in front o the Bristol Channel."

BURKE & HARE – FAIR

Fair these body snatchers certainly weren't, however, their names did lend themselves to a popular slang phrase. A Victorian child deprived of a treat given to a sibling may well have been heard to say...

"That's no Burke & Hare why dae I no get yin o them?"

BURLINGTON BERTY – CLERTY

Boys will be boys, and a kick about up
the park can sometimes get a bit messy.
"Wid ye jist tak a look at yersel, yer
troosrers are Burlington Berty."

BURRELL COLLECTION – ERECTION

There's nothing more enlightening than a jaunt
round Scotland's art galleries, some of which
house works of a somewhat erotic nature.
"Take a gander at this, that's some
Burrell Collection he's got on him."

BUT 'N' BEN – PEN

J K Rowling has made her fortune,
and there are many others out there

trying to emulate her success.
"Jist pick up yer But 'n' Ben and
start writing, who knows, it could
be the next Harry Potter."

CABBAGE & RIBS – HIBS

'Eat up your greens!' our parents always told
us as they placed a plate of meat and two veg
in front of us. The Easter Road famous five
from the 1950s certainly must have done
so as they went like the wind most games.
"Come on the cabbage. Ye can surely eat
these Jam Tarts up fur tea. They're rubbish!"

CAIRNGORM – STORM

Many a climber has been caught out by the
wonderful Scottish climate over the years.

The only thing to do is to make sure the mountain rescue team phone number is keyed in to your mobile before you set off! "Nae bother, I'll pick ye up. It's a right cairngorm the night."

CALEDONIAN MACBRAYNE – RAIN
Scottish island life can be a very damp experience. Having to travel by ferry can leave you just a little windswept and interesting-looking. "Ma Callard & Bowsers are soaked richt through wi aw that Caledonian Macbrayne."

CALLARD & BOWSERS – TROUSERS
Behind every man there's normally a very strong-willed woman.

"Aye it's nae difficult tae see wha's
wearin' the Callard & Bowsers
in that Robert the Bruce."

CAMERON TOLL – HOLE

If you're not canny with the credit cards
you can dig yourself a great big one.
"Did ye see the size of that Cameron Toll
in the grund? Ah could park a bus in it."

CAMPSIE HILLS – PILLS

Can munro bagging give you 'tense nervous
headaches' as the advert used to say?
"Gonnae dish oot a coupla yon
campsie hills. Ma heid's absolutely
thumpin' by the way."

CAPTAIN KIDD – LID

This is from the days when the word pirate
didn't mean a dodgy video. I wonder if they
used to get ship rage sailing on the high seas.
"I widnae go in there if ah were you.
He's flipped his Captain Kidd."

CARAMEL LOG – BOG

I'm sure we all know which one we prefer.
"Ah'd see the doctor if ah were you.
That's four times you've been tae
the caramel log the night."

CARNOUSTIE – FOUSTIE

Just occasionally Scottish cuisine can
fail to live up to expectations.

"A widnae touch yon sponge cake, it looks a we bit Carnoustie tae me."

CARSTAIRS – FLARES

At one point in the 1970s there were many parents who thought the younger generation had gone completely mad. "Whit a state ye are, an' jist look at the size o' yer Carstairs, ye'll trip o'er as soon as ye're oot the front door."

CATHCART – FART

Lying on the White Cart Water just
south of Glasgow, you can really
sail close to the wind here.
"Ah wid skidaddle oot o' here.
A'm just aboot tae Cathcart."

CATHKIN PARK – DARK

When the lights finally went out
on Third Lanark in 1967 probably
nobody realised that one day they'd be
remembered by way of a slang reference.
"Turn oan that light it's too Cathkin
Park tae see onythin' in here."

CHAMOIS LEATHER – BLETHER

Women may be from Venus and men
from just outside Mars, but surely the
one thing they all have in common
is the ability to natter. Tongues
were given for various reasons.

"You sit doon there hen, I'll grab the
bevvies and we'll hae a right guid
chamois leather, warts and all."

CHARLES MCINTOSH – WASH

The original Big Mac certainly
knew how to stay dry.

"Look at ye, yer absolutely mockit. Go and
get a Charles McIntosh right this minute."

CHARLES RENNIE MACINTOSH – POSH

Scotland's most celebrated architect and interior designer certainly had flair, style and panache in abundance. The burning question was, how plummy did he sound?
"Ye sound that different on the phone, affy Charles Rennie."

CHARLIE NICHOLAS – MISS

Whether scoring on the pitch or off it, this was one thing that he very rarely did.
"How did ye no' score? That wiz the worst Charlie Nicholas ah've ever seen."

CHIC MURRAY'D – BURIED

The laconic Glaswegian comic was a master of delivery and was greatly admired by his peers. He could certainly never have been accused of dying a death on stage.

"He's no' fir that ashes cairry on, he wants tae be Chic Murray'd so he does."

CHIC MURRAY – CURRY

The second slang reference for Scotland's finest comedian, who has a special place in our hearts. His name will live on forever not only because of the laughs he gave us but also for lending his name to our favourite Saturday night takeaway.

"Noo what did a dae wi' they indigestion

tablets? That Chic Murray's comin
back oan me something' rotten."

CHIC YOUNG – DUNG
No one dishes the dirt on Radio, some of
which positively stinks, quite like Chic.
"'am just off up the high field tae
spread some Chic Young."

CHIVAS REGALS – SEAGULLS
A visit to any village on Scotland's
coastline will bring much pleasure
but little chance of a lie-in.
"Those Chivas Regals hud me up
again at 5am, whit a racket."

CHORUS & VERSE – ERSE

Parents of yesteryear were certainly not averse to dealing with tantrums by using the dreaded slipper to deal with fractious tempers. Today's parents however, must be seen to show patience in abundance.

"If ye dinnae stop that greetin', this haun o' mine is gaun' right across yer chorus."

COLLIE DUG – MUG

Bearded, border or rough may all be magnificent looking canines. Used in another context, they can have a special meaning for an ex boyfriend.

"And another thing, the next time you look at yer collie dug in the mirror, I'd brek the mirror first."

CONAN DOYLE – BOIL

Holmes and Watson wi spots on!

CORNED BEEF – DEEF (DEAF)

After years of factory toil and before
ear plugs were a statutory requirement,
this is how a woman would have
explained her husband's predicament.
"Ye'll get boy scout oota him,
he's corned beef noo."

COWDENBEATH – TEETH

To be a supporter of the Fife football
team, otherwise known as the Blue Brazil,
you really have to be able to smile.
"I cannae talk for lang. I've no' got
ma Cowdenbeath in the noo."

CRAIGLOCKHART – GOCKIT

Residents of the affluent Edinburgh suburb would probably not associate themselves with general ugliness. So when describing someone who doesn't have Hollywood looks, it might just soften the blow to utter the cry:

"Have ye checked a mirror lately, yer a bit Craiglockhart."

CREAM COOKIES – BOOKIES

It's a safe bet to say that eating and gambling are a Scotman's two favourite pastimes.

"He's nae here pal, yer mare likely tae catch 'im roon the corner at the cream cookies"

CREAM PUFF – HUFF

Denying a sweet tooth his fix could
easily put him in a strop.
"That you in a cream puff again?
Stop acting like a wean."

CROOK OF DEVON – HEAVEN

When we finally depart this
earth, we generally hope our spirit
goes the right way... up.
"I, he wiz a guid man. Aye thinkin' o'
others an' no jist hissel', there'll be a place
fir him in Crook o Devon nae doot."

CULLEN SKINK – THINK

Not sure if you really like fish soup.

"Have a wee cullen skink aboot it first."

CULLODEN – SODDEN

Would Bonnie Prince Charlie
have fared better if he'd had a
golf umbrella? Probably not.

"Look at ye, ya midden. Yer absolutely
Culloden. Go and take they wet clathes aff."

CUMBERNAULD – BALD

Can it still be classed as a new town?
Hair today, gone tomorrow.

"Can ye believe it? I'm only 25 and
already gon' Cumbernauld."

CURRENT BUN – HUN

No chance of a decent pie at Ibrox, I suppose.

"This place is just fu' o current buns."

DAN DARES – FLARES

The eagle has landed. He could
have been flying too, wearing some
of the trousers from the '70s.

"Please tell me yer no' gon' oot like that.
Look at the size o' yer Dan Dares."

DANNY MCGRAIN – BRAIN

It seemed as if the marauding Celtic
fullback of the '70s and '80s could run
all day if he chose. Which was probably
why he never had time for a shave.

"Ye've got a Danny McGrain. Use it!"

DAVID STEEL – MEAL
The former leader of the Liberal party was at one time the youngest Member of Parliament, representing the Borders constituency of Roxburgh, Selkirk and Peebles. They make them tough down there so there would have been no skipping of breakfast.
"Just sit doon and eat yer David Steel in peace and quiet."

DAVID WILKIE – SILKY
Wilkie: one of the few Scots to reach sporting nirvana. Somehow, I don't think the training would have been a smooth ride.

"He's a right patter merchant. He's that David Wilkie, he could charm anyone."

DEACON BRODIE – BOADY (BODY)

A Scotsman is ever keen to express
the virtues of the opposite sex...
"Yon dancer at the social club, whit a
Deacon Brodie she hud oan 'er."

DEEP FAT FRIER – LIER

Our record on health over the years
certainly leaves a lot to be desired,
going by the copious facts and figures
relentlessly spewed out by the Health
Department. Is our nation really that bad
or is the Department a deep fact frier?

"Who are you trying tae kid?
Ye've been doon that boozer aw
day ya wee deep fat frier ye."

DENIS LAW – HEID THE BAW

Could be praise of your footballing ability,
but in reality means you're a balloon.
"Yer nothin' but a Denis Law!"

DES O'CONNOR – STAUNER

There's no doubt that Des could
charm the birds off the trees, but
this slang reference really has more
to do with the birds and the bees.
"Ah jist kissed her but it wis enough tae
gie me a wee bit o a Des O'Connor."

DOLLY DIMPLE – SIMPLE

Some people are blessed with greater intelligence than others. It's a case of making the most of the grey matter we're born with...

"Dinnae gie him twa jobs tae dae at wance he's a wee bit dolly that yin."

DOROTHY PAUL – FALL

Glasgow's funny woman certainly never tripped up over any of her lines.

"Watch ye dinnae hae a Dorothy on that pavement hen."

DRUMNADROCHIT – GOCKIT

Nessie must get bored trying to evade the crowds all summer long, but when

it's off-peak season, she might take a
chance and meander down the little
quaint village for a pint at the local. She
wouldn't be that stupid, would she?
"Oi, Einstein! I said 2 pints o' milk and a
loaf o' breid, no' the other way roond. Yer
no' hauf Drumnadrochit the night Sir."

DRY STANE DYKE – HIKE
Tired of being ripped off on foreign
soil, good Scots could explode like this,
though it's unlikely that the perpetrators,
when sussed, would have a Scooby
about what was being said to them.
"'am no payin' 100 euros fir that pal,
awa' an' tak' a dry stane dyke!"

DUKE OF ARGYLLS – PILES

This one might not sit easily with the
landed gentry of Scotland. However,
this common medical condition
doesn't recognise class boundaries.
"Ah need tae keep aff yon cauld stane floor
cos ma Duke O Argylls are gein me jip."

DUKE OF MONTROSE – NOSE

I'm sure the descendants of this family
line are very proud of their hooters.
"Got a right itchy Duke of Montrose.
Does that no' mean ah'm
gonnae get angry?"

DUMFRIES – JAM PIECE

Depending on your pronunciation it really
would be dumb to put your French fries
in a piece. It would taste much better
with either raspberry or strawberry.
"Maw, go and make us a Dumfries
will ye? You make it the best way."

EIGHTSOME REEL – FEEL

With these traditional Scottish dances,
it really is a case of getting up close and
personal. Love thy neighbour and all that.
"He's an animal. His Frankie
Vaughans were aw' ower me. Gieing
me a right guid eightsome reel."

ELAINE C SMITH – PISS

The Glesga funny woman has extracted
it in large amounts over the years
both in her stand-up routine and
as the indomitable Mary doll.
"Ah hope yer no' takin' the
Elaine C, because ah'm no' in
the mood fur yer cerry oan."

ELSIE TANNER – WANNER

The Scottish male fraternity are not averse
to a good drink down at the local and when
challenged to the ultimate drinking challenge
they don't like to be seen as second rate.
"Nae probs man, a'll doon that
pint in an Elsie Tanner."

EMMA JANE STIRLIN' – BIRLIN'

The St Judes Infirmary songbird has been
known to rattle a few cages, and her budgie
likes nothing better than to dance around
the living room to a good ceilidh tune.
"That Strip the Willow's no easy by
the way, an' ma heid's thumpin' wi' aw
that Emma Jane Stirlin' aroon".

ERIC LIDDLE – DIDDLE

A most principled man, he followed
his beliefs and won an Olympic gold
medal. He most certainly would not
have raided the leckie meter.
"Whit ye playin'at? I hope yer no'
on the Eric Liddle again."

FALKIRK WHEEL – SPIEL

This modern day momentous feat of engineering has certainly got the local bairns talking in their droves. By reconnecting the Union and Forth & Clyde canal, it's hoped that river trade will take place between Glasgow and Edinburgh just as it did many moons ago. Could come in handy if you've missed the last train home. "Stop talking rubbish man. Ah ken ye were back oot wi' her. I've hud enough o' yer Falkirk Wheel."

FAT BOAB – JOAB

Unemployment figures often make the news, especially following the sad demise

of our great mining and ship building
industries, but Scots are nothing if not
resilient in the face of adversity.
"Twenty years doon Bilston Glen, that
wiz a tough life, noo 'ave got a Fat Boab
servin' pints doon at the Legion."

FORFAR BRIDIES – SIDIES (SIDEBURNS)

The king of rock 'n' roll did once
step off a plane and onto Scottish
soil but I understand he never quite
made it to the home of the bridie.
"Mind whit yer daen wi yon clippers, I
dinnae want tae lose ma Forfars."

FORRES MECHANIC – PANIC

It always pays to keep a cool head in critical situations, even when it looks as if the wheels are about to come off.

"A goat ma sel' intae a richt Forres Mechanic when ma tyre blew oot in the snaw jist afore Soutra Hill."

FRANCIE AND JOSIE – DOZY

An IQ test was never going to be a top priority for either of them.

"For God's sake man, listen to whit am sayin'. Yer no hauf Francie and Josie the night."

FRANKIE VAUGHANS – HAUNS (HANDS)

An impressed foreman talks up the talents of one of his best labourers.

"Aye Jackie's a great lad, no frightened tae get his Frankie Vaughans dirty."

FRED MCAULEY – BROLLY

The ex-accountant funnyman keeps dry these days, as he hosts a regular morning slot on Radio Scotland. Does he take a rain cheque?

"If ye think a'm gon' oot in that wi'oot a Fred McAuley ye've got anither thing comin."

FULTON MCKAY – TIE

The incomparable Mr McKay in Porridge

was never seen without one. Trying to combat Ronnie Barker's Fletcher, he probably wished he could wring one round his neck. "You gon' oot? Looking fair dandy wi' yer tin flute and Fulton Mckay."

GALASHIELS – WHEELS

Although set in beautiful countryside, it's still advisable to take your car to get there. The A7 can be a long road on foot. "Ah'll leave it up tae you tae set the Galashiels in motion."

GARNGAD – BAD

A heavy industrial area, it suffered more than most from pollution in the early part of the last century. Unlike New

York, it wasn't so good and even changed
its name to Royston. The town was
practically rebuilt after World War II.
"It's lookin' Garngad the night boys.
5-0, and it's only hauf time."

GARY GLITTERS – SKITTERS

You can pay a dear price for a
night of booze and Balti.
"Vic'll no' be oot o' there in a hurry. He's
got a richt dose o' the Gary Glitters."

GAS COOKERED – SNOOKERED

If your supply is cut off for some reason,
you'd better have a microwave for backup or
else you're up the creek without a palate.
"Ah dinnae get paid until next Friday so

that's me totally gas cookered until then."

GASKET JINT – PINT

As one mouth closes, another one opens.
"That's me feenished, so see you
doon the pub. There's a gasket
jint wi' ma name oan it."

GATEHOUSE OF FLEET – SLEET

In the winter, kids in Scotland long for
snow, as it often means a day off school
and maybe a decent snowball fight.
Sadly, more often than not the Scottish
weather fails to deliver the goods.
"It's no' quite snaw yet, still
jist Gatehoose o' fleet."

GORDON RAMSAY – PANSY

An all-consuming career he may have,
but a spot of gardening might just bring
down the blood pressure. Mind you, he'd
probably grow self-raising flowers.
"Get aff yer feet and stoap acting
like a big Gordon Ramsay."

GORDON STRACHAN – CRACKIN'

The flame-haired midfielder provides
the slang reference for praising
the hot food at Parkhead.
"These pies are Gordon
Strachan by the way."

GREGORY'S GIRL – TWIRL

Bill Forsyth's masterpiece might not initially
appear to have much in common with
Bruce Forsyth. However, when going out
for an evening a Scottish Bruce might say:
"Hey Anthea, yer lookin' gorgeous by
the way, gie us a Gregory's Girl."

GRETNA GREEN – KEEN

If you were going to get married,
you'd have to be, wouldn't you?
"Is that aw the thanks ah get? Ye could
at least be a bit mare Gretna Green."

GREYFRIARS BOBBY – JOBBIE

The famously faithful dog, who in his day
would no doubt have been responsible
for fouling the pavements in and around
the Grassmarket area of Edinburgh.
"Watch oot pal, ye're aboot tae
staun oan a Greyfriars Bobby."

HAGGIS & NEEPS – CREEPS

I suppose a sheep's stomach doesn't really
sound the most appetising of meals.
"There wiz jist somit aboot him. He
didnae hauf gie me the haggis."

HAMILTON ACCIES – PACKIES

Not PC, like many examples of rhyming

slang, though appreciated by the vast majority
of the nation for staying open all hours.
"Gonnae nip doon tae the Hamilton
Accies an' get us a pint o' milk will ye."

HAMISH MACBETH – DEATH
This Highland bobby was always
full of life, but as they say, all good
things must come to an end.
"Aye, Tam wisnae feelin' too hot
last nicht, he wiz lookin' like
Hamish Macbeth warmed up."

HAW MAWS – BAWS
Some balls are held for pleasure, and some
of course for charity, but every now and
again, some are held in extreme pain.

"Aye he's takin' a sore yin, right in the haw maws judgin' by the look o' him."

HIELAN DANCER – CHANCER

To be considered a true Scotsman, you can't take the risk of being rumbled as a fly by night.

"He's got three wumen oan the go at wance. Whit a hielan dancer."

HIGHLAND COO – SPEW

Have you ever been alone in a field with one of these beasts? It's enough to make you sick to the stomach.

"Ah telt ye no' tae hae anither Vodka. If you Highland coo o'er ma carpet, ah'll lether ye."

HIGHLAND FLING – SING

This traditional Scottish dance was performed at the end of victorious battles by male warriors. Its slang, modern-day version is now shown on TV on a Saturday night, when performers usually get to murder a choice of songs.

"Who's she kiddin'? She can Highland fling as much as she can fly in the air."

HIGHLAND JIG – WIG

Overheard in a local hostelry, an observant drinker points out the pitfalls of sporting an ill fitting hairpiece!

"There's nae Stewart Grainger that he's no' wearin' a Highland jig."

HILLBILLY – CHILLY

Too many nights out in the woods will
freeze your duelling banjos off.

"Isnae hauf hillbilly the night sir.
That's the motor frozen awready."

HOLYROOD – MOOD

A cost of over £400m would surely be
cause enough for anyone to be in a strop.

"Whit's wrang wi' you? Ye've been
in a Holyrood aw day."

HOOSIE FRASER – RAZOR

Selling everything bar the kitchen sink, you'll
just have to find somewhere else to shave.

"Ach, ah don't believe it. Ah've no'

packed ma hoosie fraser."

IAN RANKIN – TANKIN'

The Edinburgh novelist's most famous
creation, Inspector Rebus, has certainly dealt
with a few hard men in his fictional career.
How would he fare though if his author one
day decided to give him a literary doin'?

"Jist as weel fir you that ah dinnae
believe in violence or else ah'd gie
ye a right guid Ian Rankin."

INSPECTOR TAGGART – HAGGARD

Strathclyde's finest saw more murders than
I'm sure he ever dreamt of. It's certainly one
way of getting grey hair and worry lines.

"Aye, ah think the joab must be getting' tae him. He's looking a bit Inspector Taggart these days."

INVERGARRY – CASH 'N' CARRY

Might be a bit quicker to nip in to your local corner shop, don't you think?
"Mind the shop fir me the noo, that's me awa' tae the Invergarry."

INVERNESS – STRESS

After travelling on the A9 to get there, the chances are you'll need a few extra Valium.
"Whit a day ah've hid. Ma Inverness levels are through the roof."

IRN BRUS – SHOES

Our other national drink apparently has
special healing powers for those of us
who've had one too many the night before.
A good pair of comfy loafers may make
the falling down process a bit less likely.
"Wid ye pit yer irn brus back oan,
yer feet are absolutely stinkin'."

IRVINE WELSH – BELCH

Trainspotting never used to be like this.
"That chocolate cake disnae hauf
come back on ye. Ah've don' notin'
but Irvine Welsh aw nicht."

ISLA ST CLAIRS – STAIRS
The singer, TV presenter and
actress's career has simply escalated
since The Generation Game.
"Dinnae speak tae me like that. Get up
they Isla St Clairs and get tae yer bed."

ISLE OF BUTE – MUTE
The peace and serenity of this jewel on the
Firth of Clyde could leave you speechless.
"Oh, so ye've lost yer tongue noo. Yer
playin' the Isle O' Bute card are ye?"

ISLE OF SKYE – THIGH
No man, they say, is an island, and
life's relationships can often take their

toll. Just remember one thing, never overstep the mark on a first date.

"It wiz goin' really well wi' Julie, then ah went an' ran ma Frankie Vaughans up her Isle O' Skye an' she just flipped."

JACK & JILL – KILL (LAUGHING)

Tumbling down a Scottish hillside is no laughing matter, yet it's funny how often someone else's misfortune can make you snigger.

"Look at that pair, they're getting their Jack & Jill right enough."

JACK MCCONNELLS – HONELS

A politician's life is a bit like riding a bike. You hang on for dear life and just

hope the wheels don't come off.
"Ah'm goin' tae nip doon tae the
B&Q. Ah'm needin' some new Jack
McConnells fir the cupboard doors."

JACK VETTRIANO – PIANO
This artist's superb paintings are synonymous
with glamorous women in smoke-filled
rooms. It would be no surprise if Jack himself
had tried to woo his lady by knocking
out a romantic tune on the ivories.
"Go on, ye can knock oot a wee melody
on the Jack jist afore the bells."

JAGGY NETTLE – KETTLE
Who knows, maybe there's a homeopathic
recipe for tea with a sting in it.

"Ah'm gasping fir a brew love.
Gonnae pit the jaggy nettle oan."

JAM TARTS – HEARTS

Founded in 1874, the maroon half
of Edinburgh always enjoys putting
one over the Cabbage and Ribs.
"See Wayne Foster scored a beauty fir
the Jam Tarts the day, that's Hibs no'
gonnae win the cup fir anither year."

JAMES THE THIRD – TURD

Before being stabbed to death, this
unfortunate monarch's horse bolted and
threw him, leaving him badly injured.
He may also have landed on a cowpat,

adding further ignominy to it all.
"If yer no' careful, you'll hae a
James the third on yer irn brus.
It's safer to walk on the roads."

JAMSIE COTTER – DAUGHTER

'Lock up your daughters' is what they say. At
the sight of Rab C's pal, is it any wonder?
"Aye, the family's growing right enough.
W'iv 2 sons and 1 Jamsie Cotter noo."

JEELY JAR – CAR

I wonder how many ordinary ones you
would need in exchange for a porsche.
"Ah'm no' drinkin' the nicht so
ah'll jist take the jeely jar."

JIM MCCOLL – BRAWL

Have you ever been to a gardening show?
On the last day the plant sale makes a
trip to the A & E a distinct possibility.
"Whit a carry oan. Chairs wir flying and
aw sorts. It wiz a right Jim McColl."

JIM MCLEAN – PAIN

The former Dundee Utd supremo knew
how to rub people up the wrong way, but
nobody could dispute his amazing talent.
"Yer like a be'r wi' a sore heid the
day. Yer a right Jim Mclean."

JIM WHITE – SHITE

Slang derived from the unpopular TV football

pundit who sends legions of armchair fans to the loo when he's spouting off at half time. "That's it, ah'm aff fir a Jim White noo."

JIMMY KRANKY – HANKY
"Go and get a Jimmy Kranky and blaw yer neb."
Probably a well-used phrase of parents across the land, usually directed at a pint-sized one.

JIMMY RIDDLE – PIDDLE
In the days before pull-up trainer pants, little boys were always prone to the odd 'accident'. "Dinnae worry wee man, it's only a Jimmy Riddle. We'll soon hae ye sortit oot."

J K ROWLING – BOWLING

'Harry Potter and the Municipal Park Bowling Club' probably won't be the next blockbuster written by Joanne Kathleen. That's not to say that she has never played a game or two of lawn or 10 pin bowling before she hit mega stardom. She may even still do so.

"That'll be the light nights in.
Cannae wait tae get ma whites on
and get aff tae the J K Rowling."

J M BARRIE – MARRY

Trying to get your boyfriend to tie the knot can sometimes be hard work – some boys never really grow up.

"They've bin go'n oot fir 5 year noo and

he's still no' asked her tae J M Barrie."

JOCK STEIN – GREEN

With Mr Stein's managerial record,
you couldn't help but be envious.
"Ah'll be honest, when ah saw the size o'
her en-suite, ah wiz a bit Jock Stein."

JOCKS LODGE – DODGE

A quiet night out at the pub can
sometimes turn nasty.
"It wisnae much fun last night when ah had
tae Jocks Lodge aw they glasses an' chairs."

JOE LOSS – GLOSS

A woman often knows exactly how to

deflate a man who thinks he's finally got to the end of a particularly onerous task. "Whit dae ye think yer dain', yer no' finished yet, yon woodwork definitely needs anither coat o' Joe Loss."

JOE THE TOFF – OFF
Sometimes it can be difficult excusing yourself. It all depends on how you say it. "That's me fir the night. Ah'm Joff the toff."

JOHN GREIG – LEG
In his heyday for Rangers, he was powerful enough to sweep the whole of the opposing team off their feet. "Ah'm in paradise. Check oot the John Greigs comin' fi that skirt."

JOHN KNOX – BOX (As in OUT OF HIS BOX, DRUNK)

By all accounts, the Scottish Protestant leader would only have been standing on one, certainly not getting out of his.

"See ye've no' learnt yer lesson ya edjit. Oot yer John Knox again."

JOHNNY BEATTIE – SWEETIE

The now legendary Scottish all-round entertainer has shown us how we must adapt to survive. From stage to small screen, he's pretty much done it all.

"Nae mare Johnny Beatties the day son, ye'll ruin yer Bay City Rollers if ye hae ony mare."

JOHN O' GROATS – COATS

Family bust-up? Lovers tiff? Confused sexuality? Whatever the reason, everyone's said it at some time or other.

"C'moan, get yer John O' Groats oan, we're oota here."

JUDAS ESCARIOT – CERRY OOT

The demon drink can often make people do things they later regret.

"Go easy oan the bevvy man, if ye dinnae calm doon, ye'll hae tae go an' get anither Judas Escariot."

JUNGLE JIMS – TIMS

If you know your history, you'll know

that Parkhead in the halcyon days of the 1960s and 70s had a unique atmosphere, especially on European Cup nights.

"Aye the jungle jims 'ill be pleased the night, two wan against Real, no' bad."

KEN BRUCE – TRUCE

As the latest contestant gets zero on the pop music quiz, a certain amount of diplomacy is required. One wonders if the police have ever been called to an on-the-air fight?

"Right, nae mare moothing aff. Let's jist call a Ken Bruce, OK?"

KENNETH MCKELLAR – CELLAR

The popular tenor might have practised a few notes down below in his time. Also, a good place to keep the wine company. "Next time you want anything oot the Kenneth McKellar, get it yersel'! Ah nearly went ma bloody length."

KENNY DALGLISH – QUICHE

Finger food is as popular today as it has always been, the same as our King Kenny, who often left opposition defenders with egg on their face. "This buffet's braw, whit a lovely piece o' Kenny Dalglish yon is."

KILLIECRANKIE – HANKY PANKY

Absorbing the breathtaking scenery surely is the best way to pass the time? "They'll be nae Killiecrankie the night, that's fir sure. Ma heid's nippin'."

KILWINNING – LINEN
This Ayrshire town is an ideal place to dry your washing on a windy day, as long as you're not airing your dirty stuff in public. "Great, that's ma washin' machine oan the blink. How will ah dae ma Kilwinning noo?"

KING TUTS – GUTS
The diminutive concert venue has gained a cult reputation over recent years and provided a platform for many up-and-coming acts. As any live performer will testify, it takes nerves of steel to get up and perform. "Fair play tae the boy, that Karaoke

wisnae easy fir him. It took a bit
o' King Tuts tae dae that."

KINGSTON BRIDGE – FRIDGE
Commuters often curse the tailbacks
around Glasgow's main artery and need
to unwind when they finally get home.
"Go and gang intae the Kingston Bridge
darlin' and get me anither Mick Jagger."

LAWSONS OF DYCE – MICE
Wonder if Mickey and Minnie ever
eat meat or are they vegetarians?
"Right, phone the council. Ah'm no'
haein' Lawsons o' Dyce in ma hoose."

LEMON CURD – BURD

Impress your girlfriend, with a large dollop
on top of a crusty slice of brioche. The
modern day equivalent of a jam piece.

"Is that you goat anither lemon
curd? How d'ye dae it?"

LENA ZAVARONI – CRONEY

When the pint-sized singing sensation
won Opportunity Knocks back in the '70s,
she was, no doubt, suddenly surrounded
by friends she didn't know she'd had.
She would certainly have needed a talent
for spotting the duds from the dudes.

"That you awa' tae the pub fir a game
o' dominoes, Grandad. Who's goin',

jist you and yer Lena Zavaronis?"

LOCH NESS – MESS

Just because she lives here, doesn't
mean she's exempt from clearing
up after having a barbeque.
"Whit an absolut' Loch Ness in here. If
ah were you, ah'd get it sortit right noo."

LORRAINE KELLY – TELLY

The effervescent and ubiquitous TV
presenter, who also writes a Sunday Post
column, is one of our most beloved celebrities
to have emigrated over to the other side.
How much though does she get to see of her
beloved Dundee Utd on the box down South?

"Ah'm sick o' this. Another
Saturday night and there's no' a
thing on the Lorraine Kelly."

MA & PA BROON – TOON
Where exactly was the But 'n' Ben?
Hopefully not too far from the local pub.
"Just nippin' up the ma 'n' pa. No' be lang."

MALT WHISKY – FRISKY
A late night chaser can undeniably
lead straight-laced ones astray,
particularly when they don't know
their Grouse from their Strongbow.
"Ah don't know whit yer getting'
aw Malt Whisky aboot. Ye've

nae chance the night pal."

MARS BAR – SCAR

Glasgow's gangland culture is
notoriously violent. Certainly not
a world to get caught up in.
"Ah widnae mess wi' him, hiv
ye seen the size o' the mars bar
doon the side o' his coupon."

MARY QUEEN O' SCOTS – SPOTS

She is believed to have put herself about a
bit, which often led to some unexpected
rashes on the members of Scottish nobility.
"Look at yer pus man, it's covered
wi' Mary Queen o' Scots."

MICKEY MOUSE – GROUSE

Cheers big ears!

"Ah'll hae a double Mickey please. Nae ice."

MIDGE URE – DOUR

After having scaled the heights with Live Aid twenty years ago, everything else he does must just seem a trifle less exciting.

"Whit's wrang wi' yer face? Yer affy Midge Ure the day."

MUCK AND EIGG – BEG

A most desirable place to live for many, but from time to time teenagers might plead with their parents to try the big city for a change.

"She can Muck 'n' Eigg aw she wants,

but she's gon' tae school and that's it."

MULL OF KINTYRE – DIRE
Paul McCartney's song-writing abilities are undeniably beyond question but when he winged his way to the South West of Scotland, no one could have predicted that he'd pen a tune that could send a nation to sleep forever. Pure genius.

"Och, no' yon frog song again. It's totally Mull O' Kintyre, so it is."

MURRAYFIELD – GUM SHIELD
The tooth fairy could be a regular visitor to Edinburgh if they're not careful.

"Thank God ah had ma Murrayfield

oan. Did ye see the size o' that
no. 7? Whit a bruiser!"

NICK NAIRNS – BAIRNS

Celebrity chefs have become almost
permanent fixtures on our TV screens these
days, with one or two of them throwing
tantrums which wouldn't look out of place
in a kindergarten. Ready, steady, left hook!
"It's only a fitba' match that ye've
lost. Get real and stop actin' like
a bunch o' Nick Nairns."

NORTHERN LIGHTS – TIGHTS

"Och no, ah've got a ladder runnin'
richt doon the back o' ma Northern

Lights. Jist bran' new oan as weel."
Just what a girl doesn't need
on an evening out.

NORTH SEA OIL – TOIL
It's not exactly a walk in the park working in
those conditions. Crude it certainly can be.
"It'll no' be easy. There's gonnae be a
fair bit o' North Sea oil involved."

PAN BREID – DEID (DEAD)
Bread and butter is often referred to as a
staple food of life. In this slang reference
however, the opposite applies. Our
esteemed Scottish crime investigator,
Taggart, may well have exclaimed.

"Nae need tae check his pulse, he's pan breid..." as his colleagues pull another rotting corpse from the Clyde.

PARAFFIN ILE – STYLE
Fashion has always been important to Scotland's young night clubbers, but in the halcyon days of the '50s and '60s, a greater sense of occasion seemed to exist. "Hey, look at you, really pushin' the boat oot the night. Pittin' oan the paraffin like naebodies business."

PARTICK THISTLE – WHISTLE
The famous phrase 'Firhill for thrills', presumably encapsulated an era which

sadly seems to have gone off the
radar for the foreseeable future.
"Can ye no' jist play quietly instead o'
blowin' that Partick Thistle aw the time."

PAT & MICK – SICK

A day off here, a day off there, surely
no one will notice? Will they?
"He's a heilan' dancer that yin, aff Pat
& Mick again, ah dinnae think sae."

PETER GRANTS – PANTS

"See that new winger, he's
Peter Grants by the way."
Former Celtic footballer loved and loathed
in equal measure across the great divide.

PETER NICOL – PICKLE

Scotland's greatest ever squash player has certainly got himself out of some tight situations in the past. His biggest escape act to date was moving south of the border, so that now he represents England!

"Da, Ah've goat masel' in a bit o' a Peter Nicol. Any chance of lending me fifty quid until pay day."

PINEAPPLE – CHAPEL

In London, they may have to go through Strawberry Fields by banana boat and up the apple and pears to get there, but in Scotland, it's more straightforward than that.

"Right hen, that's the tea oan. Ah'll no'

be lang, ah'm jist aff tae the pineapple."

PIPES AND DRUMS – FINGERS AND THUMBS

If you have a penchant for fumbling,
then learn to play the triangle.
"Ah wiz that nervous. See lightin' ma
fag, ah wiz aw pipes and drums."

PITTENWEEM – CLEAN

Even the fish are spotless!
"We moved in last Friday and didnae
hae tae dae a thing. They'd left the
place absolutely Pittenweem."

PORTOBELLO – CELLO

It's amazing what you can find on a beach.
A bit of wood and a bit of string and you're
on your way to starting an orchestra.
"That gap between yer legs, ye
could fit a Portobello there."

PORT O' LEITH – THIEF

The waterfront has had its fair share of
vagabonds over the years but the only
pinching you'll get now is to yourself, as
you see the transformation first hand.
"Whit a wee midden. He tanned
that sweetshop in a blink o' an eye.
A right wee Port o' Leith so he is.

QUEEN O' THE SOUTH – MOUTH

The Doonhammers, like many football
teams, are often a noisy bunch. The most
vocal amongst them are often prone to that
awful affliction – foot in mouth disease.

"Ye'd better shut yer Queen o' the South pal
or ye'll end up face doon in the Annan."

RABBIE BURNS – THE RUNS

Would our favourite bard
have enjoyed a curry?

"See yon Vindaloo frae last night, it's geein'
me a richt dose o' the Rabbie Burns."

RAB C – PEE

Mr Nesbit himself probably wouldn't

be so polite but the rest of us mere
mortals might be inclined to say...
*"Gonnae let me in, 'am
burstin' oan a Rab C."*

RENFREW FERRY – MERRY

The old passenger-and-vehicle chain ferry
service came to an end over twenty years
ago. However, there still exist today two
modern replicas which are keeping up the
good work. Something to smile about!
*"That wine's gon' right tae ma heid.
Ah'm feeling a wee bit Renfrew Ferry."*

RICKI FULTON – COORTING

Mentioning one of Scotland's greatest ever
entertainers to today's youth would probably

bring blank looks all-round. It just might be slightly less embarrassing if one asked them: "Are ye Ricki Fulton tonight?"

RITA RUSK – BUSK

Any requests sir, something for the weekend perhaps? The Barber of Seville will do, thanks. "Com' oan, let's hit Buchanan street and gie it a Rita Rusk."

RIVER CITY – KITTY

The success of the programme has certainly put a cat amongst the pigeons in soaps-land. "Pit yet Frankie Vaughans in yer sky rocket. A tenner in the river city if ye don't mind."

ROBERT CARLYLE – BILE

He is renowned for his character acting, and
some of his roles are more bitter than others.
"Ah've been baulkin' aw night. Just a
bit too much o' the Robert Carlyle."

ROBERT THE BRUCE – HOOSE

No doubt about it, Bannockburn's green belt
is disappearing like everywhere else these
days, in favour of sprawling new estates.
But then, even a spider needs a home.
"Ma telly's on the blink, dae ye mind
if I com' o'er and watch the fitba'
at your Robert the Bruce?"

ROB ROY MACGREGOR – BEGGAR

This great warrior fought hard for his pound of flesh. His name though, in slang terms, refers to those who make their living in a less strenuous fashion.

"Aye ye've tae mind where ye go these days, the city centre's jist fu' o' Rob Roys."

ROYAL MILE – WHILE

If it were the Royal Yard, the impact would not be quite the same, would it?

"Hae some patience will ye? It's no' a rush joab, it's gonnae take a Royal mile, right."

SALLY MCNAIR – HAIR

Losing your curls whilst presenting

Reporting Scotland gives a new insight on the profession of newscaster. "Yer Sally needs cropped. It looks like a mulberry bush."

SALVADOR DALI – SWALLY

When you are a surrealist painter, there's a good chance that alcohol has played a large part in your artistic output. "Fancy nippin' doon tae the Red Lion for a quick Salvador?"

SCOOBY DOO – CLUE

It was always a toss up between the loveable Great Dane and his goofy pal Shaggy, as to who was the bigger imbecile. Non human beings can be

classed under this clueless category too.
"Whit ye daein' ya numpty? See you,
ah'm no jokin', ye've no' got a Scooby."

SCOTCH & WRY – CRY

If you have any sense of humour at all,
you'll have a good chuckle listening
to the Rev. I M Jolly, but every now
and then you need a good greet.
"Tam's o'er by ha'in a wee scotch n' wry
cos he's jist had his dug pit doon."

SCOTTISH BLEND – MEND

A cuppa makes all your worldly problems
disappear. That's the theory anyway.
"Feelin' a bit better noo hen.
Oan the Scottish blend."

SHALLOW GRAVE – RAVE

Burning the candle at both ends is
what being young is all about. Beware
though, you just might meet your
Maker sooner than you intended.

"Ah've no' had a wink o' sleep, that
shallow grave went oan aw nicht."

SHAREEN NANJIANI – FANNY

This popular newsreader's forename,
used on its own, is more than adequate to
represent the Scottish female genitalia...

"Ma Shareen's mingin' by the way,
'am gonnae hae tae go tae the clinic
the morra an' get it sortit oot."

SHERIFF'S BADGE – RADGE

Back in the Wild West there were no
anger management courses, no siree. More
like pistols at dawn, if you were lucky!
"Hiv ye seen him drivin'? Heid doon,
does his sheriff's badge if anyone dares
get in his way. Absolute fruitcase."

SHETLAND PONY – PHONEY

An ignoramus can be referred to
as a donkey, and the insincere also
belong to the horse family.
"Hey you ya Shetland Pony, that
mobile ye selt me is a dud."

SHINING BRIGHT – RIGHT

The lights are on but no one's home, and
some teenagers hope the mater and pater
will turn a blind eye to their gallivanting.
"Aye that'll be shining bright, yer
no' gang doon the pub wi that mob.
Yer no' even seventeen yet!"

SHINING BRIGHT – RIGHT

As long as you put on the right type
of protection, nothing cheers you
more than a glorious sunny day.
"Howz it gon' big man? Aye, magic.
Absolutely shining bright."

SINGLE FISH – PISH

The stench of urine fills the side streets
of most Scottish towns after closing
time, usually after folks have visited
the nearest fish and chip shop.
"Haud on a meenit, afore ah hae ma scran,
ah'll need tae go fir a single fish, ya bass."

SKARA BRAE – TAE

Seeing as much of the 5,000 year-old
Neolithic settlement is constructed
of stone, villagers must have stubbed
their tootsies all the time.
"Ah ya bandit ye! There's weans
toys everywhere. Ah've gon' an
hit ma Skara Brae again."

SKY BOAT SONG – THONG

In Bonnie Prince Charlie's day, there was little or no chance of catching a glimpse of a lady's under garments. My, how times have changed!

"Aye, ye could see the tap o'er Skye boat every time she bent o'er."

SKY DIVER – FIVER

Like everyone else, Scots folk often fall on hard times every now and then, with the next pay packet a long way off.

"Gonnae lend us a sky diver, ah dinnae get ma wages tae next Thursday."

SKY ROCKET – POCKET

Yes we've all been there, misplacing

the car keys just before embarking
on a fortnight's holiday!
"Ah dinnae believe it, ah must a pit
them in ma sky rocket efter aw."

SOAPY BUBBLE – TROUBLE

If that bath hasn't been run to the right
temperature for your beloved, you'll be in
dire straits. Well, or in hot water certainly.
"Ah'll tell ye wan hing. If ye dinnae
stop pullin' they faces you'll be
in right soapy bubble."

STEELY DAN – PAN (LAVATORY)

False teeth are not as prevalent in the 21st
century as they were in the middle of the
20th, however, those who do have 'wallies'

must be wary, especially when in the cludgie.
"Och no, that's me jist flushed ma
wallies doon the steely again."

STEWART GRAINGER – DANGER

I've no doubt the Hollywood legend would
be astounded to find his name used as
Jockney slang, but oddly enough it is. Here
a man comments to his pal about the size
of the stomach of a lady going past:
"There's nae Stewart Grainger
that she's no' up the duff."

TACKETY BITS – TITS

Can be every bit as comfy as a
well-fitted 36DD bra.
"Call me a male chauvinist if ye

want, but that's a lovely pair o' tackety bits ah've gottae say."

TAM O SHANTER – BANTER
Straight from the horse's mouth, Tam's mare Meg would have had many a tale to tell if only she'd been able to speak. "Dinnae mind me, 'am jist sittin' here enjoyin' aw the Tam O Shanter."

TARTAN RUG – DUG
It's the first thing a Scottie packs away when he goes on his canine picnic. It really is a dogs' life. "A cross between a Yorkie and a Great Dane! Yer ha'in me oan. That's the

strangest tartan rug ah've ever herd o'."

TEDDY BERRS – GERS

In the midst of an Old Firm game,
cuddly doesn't really spring to mind.
"Com' oan the teddy berrs, gie us a goal."

TEN BOB BITS – TITS

In slang terms, a woman's breasts are
deemed to be of greater value to a Scotsman
than to his English counterpart.
"Aye she wisnae much o' a looker but
she had a lovely pair o' ten bob bits."

TEN BOB NOTE – THROAT

Some people would rather choke

than spend their own money.

"Gonnae get us some o' they cough sweets. Ma ten bob note is rid raw the day."

THE HAMPDEN ROAR – SCORE

Picture Rampant Lions floating over a sea of tartan-clad supporters in the grand old stadium in Mount Florida. There was no mistaking the sound, as Ray Clemence will testify, when King Kenny placed the ball between his legs and into the England net. Legend has it that just as Kenny turned away to celebrate he uttered the immortal line, "What's the Hampden Roar now, Ray?"

TIN FLUTE – SUIT

As a proud father gets wind of

his daughter's engagement...

"That'll be me needin' a new tin flute noo."

TIN PAIL – JAIL

They'll just have to find some other
use for it rather than slopping out.
"D'ye want tae go tae the tin pail? Cos
if ye cerry oan like that, ye will!"

TOM FARMER – CHARMER

They say that hard work plays a big
part in any success. Mr Farmer is one
businessman who's certainly proved that
point. However, ladies should be wary
when they come across a patter merchant.
"Aye, jist keep an eye oan 'im, 'ave
heard he's a bit o' a Tom Farmer."

TONY ROPER – STOCKBROKER

Who knows, maybe the author of The Steamie has shares in a laundrette chain somewhere. The value of your washing can go up as well as down, depending on the soap powder you use.

"When ye say yer getting' dividends, diz that mean ye hiv yer ain Tony Roper, or hiv ye bin daeing a lot o' shoppin' at the Coappie?"

TOSS THE CABER – NEIGHBOUR

The slang term certainly implies something a touch more strenuous than borrowing a cup of sugar.

"Ah, we're very lucky tae hiv

such guid toss the cabers."

TRAINSPOTTIN' – ROTTEN
Heroin induced nightmares must really stink.
"He's been completely trainspottin' the
night. He's hardly touched the baw."

TURKISH DELIGHT – SHITE
Scots are renowned for their
sweet tooth and probably for their
erratic bowel movements too.
"Geeso, whae's jist done a Turkish in
the cludgie, it's rank in there!"

VARICOSE VEINS – WEANS
Children running amok could certainly

cause a few vessels to pop.

"If ye dinnae get they varicose
veins oot o' here, ah swear tae God
ah'm gonnae blaw a gasket."

WALLY DUGS – JUGS

Slang references often refer to
man's most basic instincts.

"Ma new girlfriend's a smasher
by the way, and she's got a rare
set o' wally dugs oan her."

WEST HIGHLAND WAY – GAY

Let anyone be happy to walk it,
including homophobes.

"He must be West Highland Way
right enough, dressed like that."

WHISKY GALORE – FLOOR

A heavy drinker wakes up and reflects with his flatmates on another night on the tiles...
"Ah didnae ken if it wiz New York or New Year, ah jist ended up lying doon oan the whisky galore."

WHODUNNIT – BUNNET

Everyone loves a mystery, but for today's youth the Andy Cap brigade tops the list.
"Ah bet ye've got twa packets of bacca stashed under yer whodunnit."

WILLIAM RUSSEL FLINT – SKINT

The much heralded Edinburgh watercolour artist no doubt had days when all he wished for was a regular wage.

"Ah'm sorry pal, ah cannyae lend ye
a bean. Ah'm Russel Flint masel'."

WILLIAM WALLACE – SOLACE

Whatever your problems in life are,
they surely can't be as bad as being
hung, drawn and quartered.

"Dinnae fret yersel' hen. Ye can
take William Wallace in that
ye're trying yer hardest."

WILLIE BAULD – CAULD (COLD)

The great Hearts centre forward of
the 1950s often turned up the heat on
opposition defences. His name though
lives on through a reference to the

inclement side of the Scottish weather.
"Shut that windae, it's getting a
wee bit Willie Bauld in here."

WOLFSTONE – PHONE

In a career spanning 16 years which
included playing to audiences all over
the world, it must be mighty difficult
getting them on the blower.
"Get him on the Wolfstone and tell
him tae get o'er here pronto."

All Crombie Jardine books are
available from your High Street bookshops,
Amazon, Littlehampton Book Services,
or Bookpost P.O.Box 29,
Douglas, Isle of Man, IM99 1BQ.
tel: 01624 677 237,
email: bookshop@enterprise.net.
(free postage and packing within the UK)

1-905102-73-9

£2.99

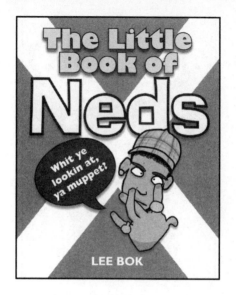

1-905102-30-5

£2.99

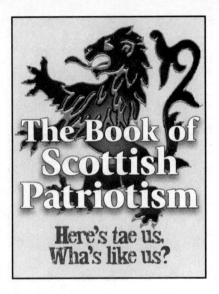

The Book of Scottish Patriotism

Here's tae us, Wha's like us?

1-905102-29-1

£4.99

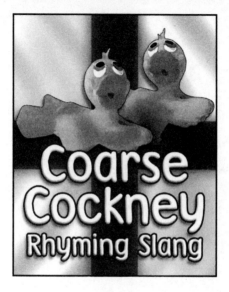

Coarse Cockney
Rhyming Slang

1-905102-78-X

£2.99

www.crombiejardine.com